Walking Between
The Raindrops

A Treatise on Trauma

~I was the prey,
I couldn't stay away~

C.W. Pickett

Mushin Press

DISCLAIMER

This publication is the opinion of the author and is not to be construed as medical advice. No treatment modality mentioned in this book is intended to be a referral. Readers are encouraged to seek a professional trauma therapist to explore treatment options that will meet your needs.

You may contact me at **cpickett@wyoming.com** if you have questions, concerns, or comments about my book. I would love to hear from you.

Dedication

To my Family
Past, Present and Future

Peace Begins with a Smile

Mother Theresa

Contents

Forethoughts

We are what we repeatedly do.
Excellence, then, is not an act, but a habit.

~Aristotle~

ACCORDING TO MARTIAL ART LORE, when a warrior comes out of a battle unscathed, he is said to have "walked between the raindrops." To march through a rainstorm of artillery, living as if death doesn't exist, requires extreme skill and enlightenment. This image perfectly describes how someone lives with an abusive partner or parent. Children avoid the abuser by keeping them happy; spouses walk on eggshells to not upset their mate.

The entire world has strayed. Everything is all about winning. Our mentality today is "if all else fails, shoot them." Get them before they get you. Top Dog. Whatever it takes.

In the end, life comes down to relationships, not how much money is in the bank. Money can't buy love.

This book is about love and relationships and treating each other fairly. It is also about abusive relationships, and the toll it takes on everyone – children, mothers, fathers, friends, and extended family. Abuse is generational. Our mothers and grandmothers tolerated abusive husbands. We pay the price with our emotional state and how we treat our bodies. We pay the price by how others treat us, and how we treat those we love the most.

The people of this world are very tense, masking symptoms of unhappiness with alcohol and drugs. Caught up in the rat race of daily living, we have lost touch with who we are. We have forgotten our self – our Soul.

This treatise on trauma is about the long-term effects of abuse, and what we can do to heal. Trauma knows no boundaries, it affects men, women, and children, and doesn't distinguish between economy or social status. Abuse and violence permeates our daily lives. This book is about understanding, not about gender, and even though the focus is on women in relationships with an abusive men, there is information here for everyone.

To resolve our trauma and prevent it in others, we need to first understand and accept our personal lot in life. Women in abusive relationships find it hard to break free. Why can't she walk away? Why does she go back? If she leaves the guy she's with she often finds another just like him. How many times does she get slapped, beaten, and put down before she's had enough? Why does she stay?

Every time she gets slapped we say, "Too bad. When will she ever learn? She's such a victim!" When we look at the heart of the matter, when we view the situation through the woman's lens, there is a different picture. Here is the chance to open our eyes to the real reasons women stay in their abusive relationships, day after day, year after year. Pure stubbornness, resilience, love, loyalty – the kids.

<u>Society</u>:   Institutions, agencies, and individuals.   These entities contribute to the family dysfunction.   Well-meaning gestures often make the family situation worse.

<u>Abuse</u>: Overpowering, misuse of, or taking advantage of a human, substance, or object.

Abusers are abusers in all levels of society. The bully doesn't just bully one little child on the playground. He bullies everyone around him.   The playground and the family are the training grounds for bullies.   Here children learn what works and what doesn't, perfecting controlling behaviors through trial and error. Here they practice the behavior that gets their victims to grovel at their feet, to hang their heads in shame. Bullies learn how to make things go their way, not through kindness and compassion, but with meanness and manipulations.

We encounter abusers in our everyday life. The police officer with power too big for his head. The politician exploits the system to fit his personal agenda. The neighbor. The boss.

It needs to be said.   We are all abusers, in some form or another. How did we become so immune to other's feelings? How did we lose respect for other people's values? When did we stop contributing the happiness of those we love?

If one person, or one family, can heal from their trauma, this book has met its goal. If one individual begins the change, another will follow, and soon there will be a Revolution. A Revolution of treating one another with kindness and respect.

In the next pages, we will look at a different point of view about abuse. You will see how childhood perceptions control our choices as adults and how these perceptions also affect how we deal with bullies, bosses, and husbands. Because of this, we have lost touch with our nurturing natures. We make wrong decisions, pick incompatible spouses, and rule our lives with fear.

The solution is not hopeless. We are not helpless to change it. Once we understand why we do what we do, this cycle of abuse can end. Abuse is generational, and it must stop.

With me. With you.

But first comes understanding - of why women stay.

Why women stay

In his book, *The Gift of Fear and Other Survival Signals that Protect Us from Danger,* Gavin de Becker explains that when a woman is repeatedly beaten, her fear mechanism is dulled to where she takes risks in stride that others would consider extraordinary. The relationship between violence and death no longer registers with her.

How does a woman feel that living under a brutal threat does not justify leaving? Forced not to resist is especially damaging because it de-programs the instinctive reaction to protect the self, and a battered woman believes she is not worth protecting. Beaten by a "loved one" sets up a conflict between two instincts that should never compete: the instinct to stay in a secure environment (the family), and the instinct to flee a dangerous environment (the family). As if on a seesaw, the instinct to stay prevails in the absence of concrete options for leaving. Getting that lopsided seesaw off the ground takes more energy than many victims have. And so, she stays...

The Rape of the Sabines

THE KING GAVE THE SIGN FOR WHICH THEY'D SO EAGERLY WATCHED.

PROJECT RAPE WAS ON.

UP THEY SPRANG, THEN WITH A LUSTY ROAR,

LAID HOT HANDS ON THE GIRLS.

AS TIMOROUS DOVES FLEE EAGLES, AS A LAMBKIN

RUNS WILD WHEN IT SEES THE HATED WOLF,

SO THIS WILD CHARGE OF MEN LEFT THE GIRLS ALL PANIC-STRICKEN.

NOT ONE HAD THE SAME COLOR IN HER CHECK AS BEFORE –

THE SAME NIGHTMARE FOR ALL, THOUGH TERROR'S FEATURES VARIED:

SOME TORE THEIR HAIR; SOME JUST FROZE WHERE THEY SAT;

SOME, DISMAYED, KEPT SILENCE; OTHERS VAINLY YELLED FOR MAMMA:

SOME WAILED; SOME GAPED;

SOME FLED; SOME JUST STOOD THERE.

SO THEY WERE CARRIED OFF AS MARRIAGE BED PLUNDER:

EVEN SO, MANY CONTRIVED TO MAKE PANIC LOOK FETCHING.

ANY GIRL WHO RESISTED HER PURSUER TOO VIGOROUSLY

WOULD FIND HERSELF PICKED UP AND BORNE OFF REGARDLESS.

"WHY SPOIL THOSE PRETTY EYES WITH WEEPING?" SHE'D HEAR,

"I'LL BE ALL TO YOU

THAT YOUR DAD EVER WAS TO YOUR MUM."

~Ovid~

Art of Love~

Chapter 1

In the Beginning

Early western tradition tells us the Roman civilization began without women. The founder of Rome, Romulus, and his brother Remus were sons of an Alban princess, Ilia, and the god Mars. Abandoned as babies, they were nursed by wolves and brought up by the shepherd who rescued them. When Romulus discovered his royal birth, he left the shepherd band to found a new community on the Palatine Hill overlooking the Tiber River. This city was eventually called Rome. To increase the numbers of his soldiers, Romulus granted asylum to fugitives from surrounding communities. The Sabines, neighbors of Rome, were reluctant to unite with Romulus. In retaliation, he and his men invaded the villages of the Sabines, took their daughters by force and made them their wives.

~Women in the Classical World~

ANCIENT HISTORY OF THE WESTERN world has its teeth sunk deep in the confines of violence. If the preceding account is true of how the founders of Rome acquired women to produce their offspring, violence has been a mainstay of our society since its inception.

It was the custom in ancient cultures for the men to go to war and the women and elderly stay behind to defend their homes. In many cultures, the girls trained in the combat arts beside the boys and continued to train through adulthood. Invaders thought villages empty of men were easy prey, but found the women and elders of the villages to be mighty adversaries.

Women are graceful and deadly practitioners of the martial arts. Excavations in the areas of China, north to the steppes of

Russia, and south to the Mediterranean Sea, are uncovering artifacts of women buried with horses and weapons of war. The Amazon woman was a myth Roman fathers used to keep their daughters in line. Through the story line of the unladylike warriors, Roman girls were forbidden to dream of the independence the Amazons represented.

It is difficult to unscramble fact from fiction through the rubble of history, myths and preserved bones, but we recognize there once was a society ruled by women. A society ruled in peace, where the women were warriors for the sole purpose of protecting her tribe, and keeping her family from harm. Like any other animal, a woman will fight to the death for her child. The warrior woman kept her weapons of war sharp and ready to use, but she preferred to tend the fires rather than fight the enemy.

Unfortunately, societal pressures have trained women to ignore this necessary skill of survival. When a woman reacts in a hostile manner, she is called aggressive, bitchy, and hysterical. This picture clouds our perception of being assertive. Along the way, women become weighted down by family and husbands who do not support them. The compromises she makes for her marriage are too demanding, and she loses her sense of self – her ability to defend herself – except through words of anger.

What does modern-day reactions and socialization have to do with the beginning of Western society and the Rape of the Sabines? Consider the psychological implications these unions must have had on the women and their children. It doesn't take a long step out on a limb to conclude our ancestors were hardwired the same as we are. Our brains are attuned to react to violence. Rape is the ultimate violent act. The Sabines were raped and ripped from their homes. From what we know today about the biology of violence and how it affects our neural development, it is a simple process of logic to discern the effects this single violent act has had on society's future generations.

If western society was founded on disrespect and disregard for other human beings, then this is the cycle of violence that must be broken. Since the founding of Rome in 753 B.C.E., our society has carried the seeds of violence. How do you break a 2700-year-old cycle?

Ovid was born in 45 B.C.E., and his poem, *The Rape of the Sabines,* was written 700 years after the fact. How accurate are stories that are written down after hundreds of years of oral tradition?

Even though the stories may change somewhat in content, the story line remains the same. An unchanging story line carries the ring of truth. Our ancestors were careful to pass the accuracy of their history on as best as they could through stories, music, and art. If this is a true story of the beginning of Rome, then deeply runs the River of Violence.

****

How People Will Like You

1. Be genuinely interested in them.

2. Smile.

3. A person's name is the sweetest and most important sound in any language – use it often.

4. Be an effective listener - Encourage others to talk about themselves.

5. Talk in terms of the other person's interest.

6. Make the other person feel appreciated – and do it sincerely.

~Dale Carnegie~

~How to Win Friends and Influence People~

****

Chapter 2

The Cycle of Childhood

If a child lives with acceptance and friendship,
He learns love is in the world.

~Dorothy Law Nolte~

WORDS OF WISDOM FOR RAISING A CHILD, a quote worth hanging on your wall and reading often. Children learn what they see and hear, sponges soaking up every sight and sound, storing the information in their busy brain. As they grow, these impressions form their personality and their view of the world.

Worldview: An individual's perception of life. How do you sort out information, what ideas do you reinforce and model, what is your personal neurological makeup? These factors contribute to your worldview.

Where do we get the ideas of how we perceive our world? Possibly from the moment an infant is conceived; definitely from our first impressions at birth. Perceptions begin with this first moment of awareness. As we continue to grow, we integrate information and form opinions in ways which affect our neurological makeup.

Neurology: The electrical pathway in the body that drives senses and physical reactions. Societal and parental expectations condition the neurological system to respond in a certain way.

Living in a world that strives for "perfection" further shapes a child's personality. The perfect job, the perfect family, money in the bank, new cars in the driveway. Our perfect life. No smoking, drinking, or lascivious sex. Be sure to exercise and eat right! From childhood, we are taught to strive for perfection. We expect to have Straight-A grades, a great body, shining white teeth, gorgeous hair.

Beneath those expectations lie guilt. We strive for nebulous states of perfection; feeling guilty because, in our mind's eye, we will never meet those high standards.

Imagine how a child feels who is never encouraged, never told she is loved, living in a house of abuse: Drugs, alcohol, and each other. Most of us lived on the spectrum of an imperfect childhood – it could have been better, and it could have been much worse.

What happens to the brain when a child lives under "less-than-perfect" conditions? What happens to the child who is repeatedly put down, slapped down, shut down? Instead of feasting on happy memories, these children become locked in a life of horrors.

A child from an abusive home becomes vigilant and diplomatic, never knowing the consequences of a gesture, a facial expression, or a request. Sometimes the parent receives a gift of flowers affectionately; sometimes they dash the gift down with a shove and an outburst of abuse. Sometimes asking for a piece of gum is "a good idea," and sometimes it brings on the tirade of "proof of your horrid greediness and incorrigible lack of concern for the cost of dental care." Sometimes looking unhappy meets friendly interest, and sometimes the parent berates and punishes the child for being selfish and ungrateful. You never know.

When at school, the child worries about what might be happening to brothers and sisters at home. A battered child will wonder what she did to deserve to be born into this family situation, and tries desperately to avoid the abuse she keeps getting.

A child may feel she is a burden to her parents, and know they feel the same way. At times, the child savagely hates her parents, but tears easily come because "they didn't mean to," or "they are just having a rotten day," or "I should have been more careful."

A child living in an abusive home wishes there was someone gentle who cared, someone to listen and understand. However, if the subject ever came up, she would defend her parents loyally, because she loves them, and she needs to believe they love her.

There is much discussion about adverse childhood experiences (ACES). A ground-breaking study funded by Kaiser Permanente began in 1995 and surveyed about 17,000 participants. The research sorted out a child's exposure in the home to such things as psychological abuse; physical abuse; sexual abuse; substance abuse or mental illness of a family member; abusive treatment of the mother; criminal behavior of household members; and a living situation with emotional or physical neglect.

15

By tracking the participant's mental and physical health outcomes over time, the researchers determined chronic and debilitating conditions are a result of adverse experiences as a child. An individual who experiences four or more of these factors during childhood has a greater risk of psychological and medical problems as an adult. The study found adults abused as children had higher incident rates of:

~ Alcoholism, alcohol abuse, and illicit drug use
~ Lung disease, heart disease, and liver disease
~ Depression
~ Risk for intimate partner violence
~ Multiple sexual partners
~ Sexually transmitted diseases
~ Unintended pregnancies
~ Tobacco use
~ Suicide attempts and suicide

Adverse childhood experiences relate to risky behaviors in children and teens, including pregnancy, suicide attempts, tobacco use, sexual activity, and illicit drug use. The higher the number of ACEs in an individual, the higher the number of chronic and co-occurring health conditions.

A parent is a child's first influence. Parents are where all perceptions and early experiences begin. Parenting is not simple by any means, but as difficult as it is, parenting is the single most important job on this planet.

Parents and the public shape perceptions and behaviors; the things that dictate how the child views daily life, how she sets boundaries, and how she deals with others. To stop the cycle of abuse, we must stop now, at this moment, mistreating our little kids. Life is hard enough as it is. Adults must stop giving children reasons to have demons.

A child who lives with tolerance, encouragement, praise, fairness, security, approval, acceptance, and friendship learns there is love in the world. It is the job of the parent to ensure these are the qualities of living they are giving their children. If each parent took full responsibility for these young lives, this world would be a much better place.

****

Teenagers who feel loved and connected to their parents have a significantly lower incident of teen pregnancy, drug use, violence, and suicide. Bonding between child and parent overrides factors traditionally linked to problem behavior: living in a single-parent home or spending less time with the child. The degree of connections that teenagers feel with parents and teachers is the most important determinant of whether they will engage in risky sexual activity, substance abuse, violence, or suicidal behavior.

~1999 Study of the University of Minnesota~

****

This key defines the parenting styles discussed on the next page:

Responsiveness – How the parent interacts with the child. Is the parent affectionate and attentive (high), or cold and dismissive (low)?

Demand – The rules and enforcements that are in place. Does the parent expect instant obedience (high) or do they give random orders with no intent to follow through (low)?

Parenting Styles

Authoritative - The Ideal Parent
High Responsiveness
High Demand
Expects mature behavior
Sets and enforces standards
Two-way communication
Uses behavior control, not psychological control

Authoritarian - The Controlling Parent
Little Responsiveness
High Demand
Does not give positive emotional encouragement
Exerts considerable control to conform to rules
One-sided communication
Little affection
Behavior and psychological control
The drill sergeant, "Because I said so!"

Permissive/Indulgent - The Lax Parent
High Responsiveness
Low Demand
Little behavior control
Encourages, and uses, childish behavior
Expressions of anger and aggression

Neglecting/Uninvolved/Dismissing - The Absent Parent
Low Responsiveness
Low Demand
Gives little time or attention
Parent-centered
Hostile or negative commands
Uses power assertion and little explanation

****

How to protect your child with bonding

1. Spend 20 minutes each day doing something your child wants to do – keep it positive.
2. During this time, no parental commands, questions, or directions.
3. Notice as many constructive behaviors as you can.
4. Do more listening than talking.
5. Use the time to build a relationship with your child, not as an opportunity to discipline behavior.

****

Chapter 3

Bullies, Bosses, and Husbands

A man without a smiling face should not open shop.

~Chinese Proverb~

A WOMAN'S SHARP TONGUE STINGS TO THE CORE and she is apt to be emotionally abusive, shouting thoughtless words and deeds. Men, on the other hand, show their control through physical strength. Both men and women resort to that horrible soul killer: Gossip. Classed as the first deadly sin, gossip does more harm than physical violence.

Bullies thrive on the group-think mentality, promoting gossip, and spreading lies. Never acting alone, their power comes from the crowd supporting them. The more people gathered on their side, the more power they have, the stronger they come after their prey. People say, "Ignore them, walk away, don't give them your power." This advice does not heed the psychological downturn these micro-aggressions can cause.

For example, think about the girl raised in poverty who wears hand-me-down shoes. The rich girls shame her for it. Day after day she walks away, avoiding the taunts. She might steal to buy new shoes. No matter how hard she tries; the burning rage, the shame, the invalidation she feels won't stop. The poor, ashamed girl. What little she had of self-esteem begins to slip. Her fears are reinforced by teachers who "don't see it" and parents telling her to ignore the bullies. One upset on top of another. And yet, she is expected to act as if nothing is wrong.

As a young woman at her first job, she has a bully as a boss. She thought she was away from the degrading comments, and now she has a boss who takes advantage of her. The man she marries resembles the bullies at school and the boss at work. He invalidates her, puts her down, and treats her like he owns her.

With no system of boundaries, the woman avoids confrontations, bites her tongue, and hangs her head. She does not teach her children the importance of setting boundaries. She loves her husband and overlooks the distressing times. Everyone has rough spots, a dark side, including herself, and she thinks acceptance and tolerance are the keys that will bring peace to the family.

She is trapped in these relationships because her brain is stuck in survival. She has been in survival mode since she was a young child. Poverty, alone, can cause emotional problems. Not to mention the shame of having to wear second-hand shoes. Never as acceptable as her peers, no matter how resilient and determined she is to be better.

We gravitate to what we know. We pick spouses who resemble our parents. Decision-making is not nearly as conscious as we think. Often we are enticed to the man we love because he has the comfort of the personality we are used to, what we have experienced. In our choice of a mate, how much of a part does love play as opposed to familiarity? Choices are more emotion-based than what we care to admit. Sensations, emotions, and memories drive our brain. We choose what we know.

Bullies and School Shootings

After the Sandy Hook Shootings in Connecticut in December 2012, the governor of Connecticut formed the Sandy Hook Advisory Council. A study of the forty-one attackers involved in the thirty-seven school shootings from 1974 to 2012 shows every single shooting could have been prevented.

- All were males, most felt bullied, all were depressed or suicidal.
- All had access to weapons, either from the family or a relative of the family.
- The shootings took less than 5 minutes.
- The shooters talked about their plans to friends; in person, and on-line.
- Some were very popular in school.
- Each attack was planned far in advance. The boys at Columbine had their plan in place nearly two years before the incident.
- Gathering weapons were part of the planning.
- All had suffered recent losses and major traumas. One had a mother going through a divorce. She told the shooter (her child) she was going to commit suicide in front of her husband.

The shooter in Alaska was bullied for years. His bullies put notes on his back and jammed up his locker. His adoptive mother was the superintendent of the schools, and she initially reprimanded three of the students, which caused the bullying to escalate. The boy was told: "Try to ignore it." The message he heard was: Ignore it or solve the problem on your own. He solved the problem - he decided to bring a shotgun to school.

The plan escalated. The target list went from three to fourteen. The boy had never used or loaded a weapon until then. The night before the shooting, he told a friend he was bringing a gun to school the next day, she warned him against it, and she stayed home from school. A boy brought a camera to take pictures of the shooting. When the shooter walked into the school's lobby, he told the classmates, "You had better run!" He shot at the ceiling, and then shot the principal.

The Sandy Hook Advisory Council discovered that children whose needs are unmet or unrecognized far outnumber the children who are a public safety threat. About eight million children enter the system every year through adoption, institution, foster care, and of course, the legal system. There is no count of the vast number of children raised by grandparents and other kinship.

****

How to Manage Conflict

1. Conflict phobia sets relationships up for turmoil. Our fear of conflict gives people permission to walk over us, and tells them there will be no consequences for their behavior.

2. Personal power comes from standing up for ourselves and for what is right. Firmness is essential!

3. Remember, we teach others how to treat us. Conflict-seeking people push buttons to get us upset, so try not to become that person's stimulant.

4. Starve the conflict, don't feed it.

****

Chapter 4

The O.J. Syndrome

People should learn to see, and so avoid all danger.
Just as a wise man keeps away from mad dogs
So one should not make friends with evil men.

~Buddha~

NICOLE SIMPSON WAS MARRIED TO A FAMOUS FOOTBALL PLAYER, O.J Simpson. Numerous domestic violence calls to the home eventually resulted in her brutal murder. The case made national news for several years because of the notoriety and shock that a celebrity could do such a thing! Law enforcement was called to the house multiple times. They never believed Nicole, even bruised up, when she said her life was in danger. The police ignored her pleas because O.J. was a nice guy, a superstar, a pillar of the community.

How many women have been brutally stabbed, shot, raped, or left for dead by their "nice" husbands? How many women live in a trap, unable to escape, because people will not believe her when she says she is in trouble?

"Well, she could get out if she wanted to. If her life is in that much danger, she should leave." True, but to complete the thought: "I'm not getting involved, that's for sure. I've told her what to do and she won't, so she's on her own."

"She's on her own." How does she get away from someone stronger and more powerful, "on her own?" Often, even with someone to help her out, she still goes back. After multiple failed attempts, family and friends, those who were concerned, stop caring. Eventually, she is truly all by herself – or dead – like Nicole.

Nicole was a beautiful, poised, confident, and affluent woman. She mixed and mingled at events where the wealthy and famous gathered. Nicole and O.J. were a glamorous couple. What demon gripped their marriage, what dysfunction existed between them?

O.J. was a football player in the day when head injuries meant nothing. Football is a dangerous sport. The "dumb jocks," the football stars, had repeated head injuries, concussions, and impact blows. How many times in a game did this forceful jarring occur? When a player was hurt, they were expected to keep on playing – it was the manly thing to do.

O.J., the great quarterback. He was the smallest, the fastest, the smartest player on the team. The target for many massive bodies to pile on. How could he have not gotten injured? The long-term effects of head injuries are personality changes, impulsiveness, irritability, and meanness. Add alcohol and drugs, and you have a volatile mix.

People mask their symptoms in public. Other mental disorders also cause personality changes, but people with head injuries are often able to present their "public face". At parties, everyone gets drunk, who cares how someone acts? O.J. was fun to be around, he had many friends, "he was such a nice guy." Nice guys surface as the child-molester, the man the family loves to pieces. They treat their women well around friends and in public and beat them at home.

Head injuries, mental illness, and PTSD; none of these are an excuse for abusive behaviors. These conditions often carry symptoms such as aggression, irritability, and moodiness. But when someone becomes volatile, whatever the reason, it is a signal to get help and find ways to avoid this behavior.

We are responsible for our own actions, whatever our state mind. To be responsible means to fix what ails you.

O.J. had connections in the community, and the police treated the incidents as a mild argument. "Things got a little out of hand, Officer. It won't happen again." For Nicole, and too many other women, it did happen again, and again. Until they are dead.

Many women are locked in the O.J. Syndrome. Home, family, kids, security, love – their lives revolve around this person who offers so much. We promised, "till death do we part."

We make reasons and excuses why we stay. People expect women look their best and to be excellent caregivers. Nature tells us to take care of our husbands and our children unconditionally. Societies all over the world disrespect those expectations! Throughout the ages, all around the world, women are raped, slapped, and invalidated daily. Even in the 21st century, where we are supposedly far advanced socially and intellectually, it appears that emotionally we are stuck in the mindset of generations ago when this behavior was accepted.

Stress does amazing things to the brain. Ponder what it takes to live in a volatile household. Keeping the peace, trying to prevent the next blow up, getting little rest because of troubled dreams, and a brain that won't stop working. Going about the day as if nothing were wrong. How many men and women, boys and girls, go through their days, despite these feelings, making the best of it?

Making the best of it and being our best is not necessarily the same thing. Every day, we make decisions that make or break us. When the mind and body boil with stress, how can anyone make a sound decision?

****

How to be Assertive

1. Don't give into the anger of others just because their anger makes you uncomfortable.

2. Don't allow the opinions of others to control how you feel about yourself. You count.

3. Say what you mean and stick up for what you believe is right.

4. Maintain self-control.

5. Be kind, but firm, in your stance.

****

Chapter 5
Bad Choices

But love is blind, and lovers cannot see.
~William Shakespear~

EVERYONE MAKES MISTAKES. Some mistakes, no big deal. Other choices dictate how we live the rest of our life.

Mate selection. How do we choose life partners? Randomly, hormonally, spiritually, intellectually? What does intellectual thought have to do with love? Love is from the heart.

We lose our heads when it comes to loving someone by losing all thought about the (im)practicality of the relationship. Shared morals and values are the solid foundation of any relationship: Intimate or casual.

Behind every great man, there is a great woman.
Behind every great woman, there is a great man.
Behind every abusive man, there is a battered woman...

Mate selection is the cornerstone, the foundation, of our life. Our success in life depends on the people we choose to have in our lives. Picking the proper mate is the first step in team building. A supportive partner will go to bat for you, pull you up when you fall, and give you a boost up when you rise. You need supportive, helpful people in your life. The first step, a positive partner.

Negative people bring down the house. A worldview of badness permeates their behaviors and thoughts. Everyone has a dark side. Negative people live on the dark side. Negative conditioning and experiences create black, dark thoughts.

Love is a horrible judge of character. "But Mom, I LOVE him!" How many mothers have heard that from their teenage daughter? And we reply, "Honey, what do you know about love?"

What is love? Love is a personal feeling, not easy to define, except love makes us euphoric.

We are happy during the courting and the honeymoon. What happens after the newness wears off? When the comfort level rises? With increase in familiarity? Are we happy then? Now comes the work. The learning of how to live together forever.

Marriage takes a lot of work. If the couple is compatible and chooses each other because they complement the team they are building, marriage is hard work. If the couple does not have rapport, the work becomes a chore.

Once familiarity sets in, the true person comes out; the buried personality that was previously hidden. Blind love; we make the most crucial life-long decision the same way a blind man who expects to see!

If we take off the blinders of love, we can predict how a man will treat a woman in the future. People do not change, and their past speaks mountains about who they are. Even if someone makes a concerted and conscious effort, intentionally trying to change their habits, in the long term, people usually resort back to who they have always been. Basic personalities seldom change. We can correct our addictions and bad habits, but the basic way we interact with people and respond to situations will always be with us.

In a happy and contented state, the last thing anyone wants to do is look at the beloved's faults. With intimacy, the body releases high doses of oxytocin, the love hormone. Oxytocin causes feelings of happiness and contentment. It also clouds judgment. As the relationship grows, the faults become more noticeable. Too late, because the committing words "I Love You" have already been spoken.

It takes less than 30 seconds to size someone up when you first meet them. Also, it takes less than 30 seconds for us to impress them! Fortunately, most of us get past the initial scrutiny and go on to forming acquaintances, friendships, and intimate relationships.

The best way to find out about someone is by listening to what they say. What is the focus of his conversation? Who does he talk about? What does he say? How does he relate to you? Does he take over the conversation and zero in on himself? "It's all about me!" Listening gives more information than talking. Start the conversation and let him go. Team building. Is this someone you want to have as a partner for life?

Boundaries are necessary. How does this man respond to you? Does he push, never quite taking your word? Does he challenge your "no," interrupt and speak over you? Or does he respectfully hear what you have to say?

Testing the new acquaintance is okay. What does his body say? Do his actions match his words? Listen, with your ears, your brain, and your heart. Your body knows before your mind. Listen to it.

Trust your instincts. If things feel wrong, they are. The reason will show itself. Trust your gut. Hear the argument between those two little voices, the angel and the devil. "Do it!" "Don't do it!" Which voice do you trust? The best tools to use when making decisions are logic, common sense, and right-headed thinking.

When you let emotion override intellect, you head for BIG trouble. Use your head when choosing a mate. Your happy heart will follow.

Booty Calls

The most convincing promise of lasting care and fidelity is the one that is based on the sincere bond of love, not on the short-term motive of sexual pleasure.

Booty calls are a negative expression of your self-esteem. Saying no to the booty calls is the ultimate way you can show yourself and the men you are looking to date that you have self-respect.

~Lawrence and Nohria~
~Driven. How human nature shapes our choices~

Sex on demand takes away your mystery. When you bare your body, you bare your soul. You leave yourself open to emotional and physical attack when you reveal your personal life to someone who doesn't know you and doesn't care.

Sex on the first date? You do not respect yourself much, do you? Neither does he.

Respect and caring develop over time. Even when friendships click at first sight, it takes time to turn into a lifelong, meaningful relationship. Relationships start with a seed, and slowly, over time with proper nurturing, grow into the wonderfully broad green shade tree you enjoy in the evening. Growth takes time.

Without proper nutrients, nothing grows well. We cannot control everything that happens to us, but we have complete control over who is in our life. Proper mate selection reduces the prospect of living in poverty and producing undereducated children.

Women who raise their children alone are more prone to poverty than any ethnic or cultural group in the United States. The highest percentages of children living in poverty come from homes with single moms. A teenager will have her first baby, and another by someone else. Before you know it, she has 3 or 4 children with no common father. By doing this, she destines herself and her children to a lifetime of destitution.

Children build an independent safety net when they decide they cannot trust their parents for protection and nourishment. Whether they draw into themselves, or externalize it with their pick of friends, their new safety net becomes their haven. Home becomes a battleground, a survival of wits. A child lives a world of duality when they do receive shelter and protection from a trusted adult.

One day, this generation of youngsters will rule the world. How many more Hitlers, Dahmers, Stalins, and Mao se Tungs do we have to produce before we get it right?

We must stop the madness we have created. Peace on earth does begin with me. Peace on earth starts with proper mate selection. By being careful when choosing your life companion, you are ensuring your children will be safe and well loved.

Is Mate Selection in our Genes?

Natural mate selection has evolved over the ages, but genes appear to play a role in how our ancestors picked their mates. Monogamy was the accepted practice in most cultures. Women, by nature, conceived, gave birth, and nursed their infants, and tended to pick husbands that proved to be supportive fathers, food providers, and nurturing husbands with traits of intelligence, faithfulness, and wealth. Men were attracted to women who were healthy and young; who could bear many children. If a woman looked younger than her peers, her chances to successfully find a mate improved greatly.

~Lawrence and Nohria~
~Driven. How human nature shapes our choices~

****

How to Choose a Mate

1. Stay away from sex. Keep the relationship casual.

2. Listen to what he says, both verbally and nonverbally.

3. Is his past full of suffering, drama, and legal problems?

4. How was his childhood? How does he relate to his family? Is he a mama's boy? Is the family supportive?

5. How did past relationships end - are the two still friends, or did they have a hurtful, destructive breakup? Was there abuse? Was he controlling and jealous? Was he unfaithful?

6. Was he in the military? Listen to see how his experience affected him.

7. How does he treat you? Is he respectful? Or does he invalidate what you say?

8. Do you share common values and goals?

****

Chapter 6

Fear Rules Us

Get over your ugly – find your inner beauty.

~Unknown~

THE MOST COMMON EMOTION IS FEAR. As creatures of habit, most people unknowingly travel through their days guided by fear. Fear causes avoidance. Limiting beliefs, the beliefs we hold close, the reasons why we don't take risks, come from fear.

The struggle for perfection, the guilt when we screw up - all based on fear. Fear of the unknown - the future. Fear of the past - the demons.

Parents instill limiting beliefs in their child from the beginning of life. Some installations of fear are useful: "The stove is hot. Do not touch it!" "Stay out of the street. You will get run over." Most limiting beliefs are not beneficial. They often do great damage. "I am worthless." "I will never be good enough." "I am stuck in this relationship."

What governs this thinking? A careful examination of why you do the things you do will reveal the beliefs that hold you back. Words ring from childhood! "You will never amount to anything!" How many times was it said, pounded into the brain? "Mom said I am worthless. Then, I must be."

Thinking this way turns our worldview into one where we feel unable to contribute, unable to be heard, in a word - worthless.

Fear guides these feelings; fears reinforced by the thing we fear the most, put-downs and invalidation.

Deep inside, we are still the small child.

Our feelings, the ways we think, the impressions we developed as children, come out in the most inopportune moments when we are adults. As children, we learn how to make friends, how to protect our inner self, what to say and how to say it. For many of us, those skills became the tools of survival. An alcoholic father is never at his best, and when he is drunk, the kids learn to hide. When hiding is not an option, children learn diplomacy. Diplomats know the physical and verbal signs of communication – not words only. Early on, the child realizes words mean nothing, and quickly learns to watch for nonverbal signs of the gathering storm.

What happens to the fear factor when someone threatens, ridicules, or invalidates your basic human rights? Abuse hurts, deep to the soul.

Why does a bully bully? A child who is called a sissy, double dared to be tough, put down for failing, will often become a bully himself. The need for control, to never let that happen again, comes out in the same kind of cruelty to others.

We learn from those around us; parents, siblings, neighbors, peers, teachers, and others in the community. We filter what we see and hear by experiences. Negative experiences make negative screens. Happy children see the world through positive filters. Happy memories keep them smiling, and they see the happy faces.

The girl with the ugly shoes sees the world as a negative place, where people taunt and make fun, where she feels "worthless." Poverty has risks. Already our girl was at high risk for a negative worldview. The girls at school made it worse.

We gravitate to what we know - confined in our fears and in our limiting beliefs.

I find it heartbreaking and infuriating that, no matter how accomplished a woman may be, we continue to see ourselves in the diminished distortion of another's view of us, especially if that view belongs to a man with whom we are having an intimate relationship.

~Sara Ban Breathnach~
~*Something More; Excavating your authentic self*~

The Cost of Anger

Raising Defenses
Aggressive behavior only results in continued aggression

Anger and Rigidity
Leads to intolerance and inflexibility of thought
Numb, judgmental, irritable, attack mode, withdrawal, revenge
Remains in the safety of the bunker rather than risk openness

Anger and Resistance
Anger shields from hurt feelings and the fear of being controlled

Psychological Death
Loses capacity to say no, to have a choice, to make decisions

Helplessness
Depends on others to meet basic needs
Gives up personal power
Nothing seems to go right
Friends sluggish and insensitive
Loved ones unappreciative and not supportive
A sense of despair about feelings of lack of love and nurturing
Resistance and withdrawal may lead to aggressive behavior
Helplessness is self-induced – despair is unnecessary

Life slides out of control
Nothing seems to work
No one cares
Feels will never be good enough

Diminished satisfaction
Relationships are low-quality and unsatisfying

Isolation
Distant friendships
Severed love relationships

Loneliness
A cynical attitude doesn't see what help is available
Unrealistic and demanding expectations turn away support

How to Build People Skills

1. Take responsibility for keeping the relationship strong, and seek ways to improve it.

2. Never take the relationship for granted, and nurture it daily.

3. Decide what you want in a relationship. Make it happen.

4. Protect your relationship. Protect the other person.

5. Encourage positive behavior by noticing their best.

6. Keep the relationship fresh – look for new and different things to add life and vigor.

7. Frequently notice and comment on the good.

8. Communicate clearly. Listen and understand.

9. Maintain and protect trust.

10. Deal with difficult issues.

11. Make time for each other. Touch and mutual love are critical to life itself. Intimate relationships need physical love to grow.

12. Keep expectations realistic.

Chapter 7

Biology

The Voice of the Heart is always positive and loving even when it is asking us to change. It is direct and specific, empowering, grounding, centering, and relaxing. It is unwavering. It will keep telling you the same thing over and over, but it won't use your own logic against you. If it is negative and critical, it is not the voice of your heart.

~Gail Harris~

~Your Heart Knows the Answer~

EVERYTHING CONNECTS: The brain, body, and soul. When looking at life, and why we do what we do, we must look to see which system is out of balance. Medicine, psychology, and neurology try to separate our bodies from our world. Does the doctor regard the patient's home life when he prescribes a pill?

Since Sigmund Freud's day, therapists taught their clients the problem lies inside their brains. If unable to "fix" what's bothering their client, the therapist labels them as dysfunctional, or having a mental disorder – a "mental illness."

Therapy, in that realm, doesn't work at all. In the first year after discontinuing therapy, the relapse rate is nearly one-hundred percent. Once taken out of the safe environment of the therapists' office, the client goes back to the old ways of thinking.

Trauma causes severe problems. The freely-given advice – "get over it," "put the past behind you," – is physically impossible. The body remembers, but the mental memories often become lost.

This is a natural protective mechanism that blanks out terrifying experiences. Unprocessed trauma appears as pain, stiffness, and mental anguish. Living with demons from the past permeates every aspect of life. We live in our agony - we are not "survivors." People in trauma have not survived anything. They live it long after the event has passed. There must be a better way to describe the feeling.

Mistreatment in childhood often results in mental health problems as an adult. A devastating accident or war may twist a perfectly sane mind, but overall, childhood experiences significantly affect how we see the world.

We are just beginning to understand the biology of our brains. Ironically, we know more about outer space than we know about what goes on inside our heads! What makes us tick? Why do we feel and think the things we do?

When cortisol, the stress hormone, combines with the many other bodily actions, it affects everything about us. Cortisol attacks nerve endings, DNA, memory, and sleep centers in the brain.

Soldiers at war are on constant high alert. Senses scream at every stimulus causing cortisol to run at extremely high levels. With prolonged exposure, the body adapts to these changes. Once home from war, the soldier experiences high alert even at rest, because the body and brain are trained to react at a second's notice. Considering the length of a lifetime, the soldier is at war for a short time. Why, then, does war affect so many people for the rest of their lives?

Children living in abusive homes never quit the war. Daily, year after year, waiting for the other shoe to drop. Waiting for daddy to come home drunk, again. Waiting for the beatings and put-downs that go with it. On the playground at school, they wait for the bully to attack, again. Waiting - and feeling helpless.

Physical force and emotional stress meet at the back door of our emotional-control center. When least expected, the fight or flight response kicks in and the hypothalamus, amygdala, pituitary and adrenal glands respond by pushing stress hormones into the system. It takes a nanosecond for this door to swing wide open, and when it does, emotions are off and running. The traumatized brain waits to receive and welcome visitors - the demons and impressions from the past. Once this happens, before we know it, the mind/body is charged with cortisol and negative thinking.

The digestive system has a separate neurological system from the rest of the body. "Butterflies in the stomach" is the old-fashioned term placed on women before the faint. As portrayed in old movies, the back of one hand touches the forehead, and the other hand clutches the stomach. We laugh at the depiction of hysteria. As it turns out, this reaction has nothing to do with hysteria or a weak stomach. However, it has a lot to do with neurology...

Hysteria mistakenly portrays a woman's state of mind. If she is out of control, she is "hysterical." What do you call an out-of-control man? No tags for his behavior.

Sigmund Freud worked and lived in the affluent part of Vienna, Austria. His theories dominated the psychology books and the treatment of mental health for a century. His earliest writings are about resolving trauma. Girls and young women, molested by their fathers, came to him seeking help, and Freud discovered hysterical reactions were the body's response to the molestations. However, if he exposed their fathers, the bankers and lawyers, the founders of his community, his career and opulent lifestyle would be ruined! Instead, he turned his back on his patients. The undoing of 100-years' worth of women.

The twisted thinking, the burning brain; the churning gut, the burning pain; the racing heart; the feelings of panic. These normal reactions happen when the body floods with stress. Instead of saying the women of yore were "hysterical," we could say they were in touch with their bodies, unconsciously responding to what was going on inside.

Through the years, women have learned to ignore these signs. "Get on with your day and quit your crying." We have stopped listening to our bodies. We do not enjoy our femininity because to be female is to be weak and hysterical.

For centuries, women fought for freedom against man's oppression. American woman's right to vote in 1920 was only a step in recognizing the power of women, and our struggle to become equal with men has come with a price. After winning suffrage came the challenge: "If you want to live in a man's world, if you want equality like a man, fine! Then play by the man's rules." Act like a man. Don't cry. Suck it up.

****

How to Nurture Yourself

In our Puritan-based society, we have not been trained to nurture ourselves. Many of us feel deep down that if we do enjoy ourselves, we will be punished for the human need to enjoy and savor the texture of our lives. Only feeling stressed feels familiar. Becoming aware is a prelude to conscious integration at a higher level. Accepting the dignity of your inner gifts makes them real -- ized.

~Doe Lang~

~The New Secrets of Charisma~

****

Chapter 8

Are You in Danger?

A woman called the shelter late one night to ask if she could come back. As always, the first question the counselor asked is, "Are you in danger now?" The woman said no. Later in the call, the woman added, almost as an aside, that her husband was outside the room with a gun. Hadn't she just a moment earlier said she was not in danger? To her, if he was in the same room with the gun, or he was holding the gun to her head, then she was in danger.

~Gavin de Becker~

The Gift of Fear and other Survival Signals that Protect Us from Danger~

FOR 75 YEARS, RESEARCHERS OF TRAUMA have attempted to answer the question of why women stay in abusive relationships. After experiencing repeated assaults, a woman justifies the beatings and/or putdowns. Her brain and body has entered a mode where she is emotionally immune to the assaults. Over time with ongoing abuse, she will experience a full and complete collapse.

The biological answer to the question of why woman stay is referred to as the human immobility response. Dr. Peter Levine (2010), a renowned trauma expert, calls this response, "The A and 4 F's". Arrest, fight, flight, and freeze are reactions to trauma. People weave in and out of these stages, but the folding into oneself is a sign of the freeze stage. Unable to move, unmotivated for action -- locked in the confines of terror.

Arrest (vigilance and scanning of people and places)

Flight (tries to escape the threatening situation)

Fight (prevented from escaping)

Freeze (frightened and scared stiff)

Fold (collapse into helplessness)

This is the cycle of violence.

When we are terrified, or physically restrained and cannot escape, we experience trauma. Years later, triggers of the event will unconsciously bring on the same feelings of entrapment as if the experience is happening in the present. A deep numbness results, which helps to mask the pain and terror that arise from these memories.

When a woman is beaten by her husband, her world of duality causes a major conflict in her mind. She is with people she loves and wants to be with, but when the home becomes a war zone, she wants to leave. The feeling of frozen in place causes a serious internal conflict; one that many women cannot win. Once her instinctive reaction to protect herself is gone, she believes that she is not worthy of protection by anyone.

A person living in chronic trauma goes through the motions of life with little vitality or enthusiasm. The immobilization that comes from an inability to remove the threat eventually causes a state of paralysis.

Paralysis is why women stay in abusive relationships. After a time, the desire to stay overcomes the instinct to flee;

it takes too much energy to make changes. With no options in place, she remains. Risks, such as a man outside her door with a gun, is not a true threat. The longer the abuse continues, the more likely she is to miss the connection between violence and death.

With the advent of functional magnetic resonance scanning (fMRI), physicians can unobtrusively watch the brain's activity in real time. This technology proves useful in the research of trauma because now researchers can see how a brain responds to a flashback or a panic attack. They find some areas light up more than usual, and other areas show no activity whatsoever. It is interesting to note that when a person is completely shut down (in the final freeze), the brain also shuts down, with no notable activity on fMRI (van der Kolk, 2014). "My brain has left me," is not as much of a cliché as we imagined. In the case of the man with the gun, the woman missed the connection between violence and death because her brain was not registering the danger. When her brain shut down, she lost all sense of self-protection.

The A and 4 Fs
Stage 1 - Arrest (Hypervigilance and Scanning)

Rape victims who are held down, accident survivors who cannot escape, and soldiers caught in the crossfire who can only lay there and let the bullets fly overhead are constantly scanning their environment for threats. Children who are locked in an abusive home experience psychological entrapment. With senses on high alert, stimulus is seen as either a threat or an irritant.

Stages 2 and 3 - Flight and Fight (Escape)

When unable to flee the situation, to leave with dignity intact, the next self-protective measure is to fight. When someone is backed into a corner, they will fight back. If fighting isn't an option, then you must flee. When reexperiencing the trauma, the person once again feels frightened and restrained. This sense of immobility leads to the fourth phase where people often refer to the feeling as a heaviness and of being stuck; like wearing cement boots or sleeping under an uncomfortable, heavy blanket.

Stage 4 - Freeze. (Frightened and Scared Stiff)

Functional freeze. We can understand this by studying animal behavior and how they react when attacked. All species of the animal kingdom use these four immobility survival functions, including humans.

1. *Last ditch survival (play possum).* Prey that plays dead thwarts the attacker. When a grizzly bear attacks, the surprised hiker is advised to hit the ground and lay still. When the bear senses no threat, she will lumber away. A woman knows what not to say to avoid causing problems, children learn diplomacy.

2. *Become invisible.* The predator puts hard work into the hunt, but if a hunter cannot easily find its prey, it will move on to something easier to catch. Rapists will run away from a screaming woman. A child will be very still and not draw attention to herself.

56

3. *For the good of the group.* In the wild, animals will often sacrifice one of their kind so the others in the herd can escape the danger. With humans, someone is offered up as a scapegoat to save the group.

4. *A state of analgesia.* Numbing occurs so the body and mind cannot feel the pain. The event seems to be outside of the body, and is not happening to you.

Fear-potentiated mobility. Unlike functional freeze, which is a tool for survival, this presents as dissociation, or separation, from reality. An unable-to-function freeze.

As time goes on and the trauma continues, symptoms become more advanced and pervasive: Dysthymia (a vague sense of depression that rises and falls during the day); the inability to focus or function in the present; dissociation; rage, anger, and irritability. Once in this type of freeze, a person becomes lost in an anxious fog and experiences complete shutdown.

When someone gets to the point of near collapse, the psyche and body does whatever it can to prevent that from happening. Anger is an attempt at righting the wrongs committed against you. Whether striking out, or striking inward, an angry person can be devastating. A person in the final stages of freeze is no longer responding to their trauma; their minds have finally twisted out of control. After the anger, comes the collapse.

Stage 5 - Fold. (Helpless Collapse)

A wife may want to shoot her husband, she knows that is not an appropriate action, and will instead fold into herself. When an animal is in a state of the final freeze, muscles become limp, and the animal collapses as though death is imminent. A helpless resignation and a complete lack of energy set in. Overwhelming feelings of helplessness and hopelessness lead to physical and mental breakdown.

Wounds won from trauma will not heal by continually ripping open those wounds. Anyone, male or female, young or old, who has grips in this cycle of trauma has problems coping. Is it any wonder why a child trapped in an abusive home is absent-minded and irritable?

Immature minds have fewer protective factors than adults. A child's emotional development stops at the point of trauma, and often never fully recovers. Younger children exhibit hyperactivity and defiance. Mental illnesses, such as schizophrenia and depression, begin in adolescence and young adulthood. If childhood maltreatment is the precursor to mental and physical health problems in adulthood, could it be these mental illnesses in young people are nothing more than the "Fold" stage in the trauma cycle at an early age?

Children who misbehave in school are not misbehaving, they are expressing their pent-up rage and anxiety. Whether this stress comes from home life, school life, or other factors, the way to prevent this wide-spread epidemic of mental illness in our young people is to ferret out the cause of their discomfort and help them resolve it.

When the trauma is resolved, then healing can begin.

****

How to Have a Successful Life #1

1. Become friends with positive people.

2. Do what you love and the money will follow.

3. Keep your power. Use it wisely.

4. Make your own decisions. Take advice lightly.

5. Strive for harmony and compassion in your life.

6. Treat people well and they will treat you the same.

7. Cure your addictions. Stop habits that block your path.

****

CHAPTER 9

It Ends with Me

One should carefully examine the man
who people universally like or dislike.

~Confucius~

THREE OUT OF FOUR WOMEN are sexually molested at some point in their lives. Even though many women have this experience in common, it comes with shame, so no one talks about it. The stigma continues because we fight our private battles in silence. Our low self-esteem is not dependent on how society conditions us, or how we think about ourselves. Lack of self-esteem comes directly from the devastating destruction the past has had on us. When the core of our being is damaged, we experience a hollowness; a constant ache that says something isn't right.

Everything is wrong. Nights fill with dreams of terror; daytime brings fatigue and racing thoughts. We mask our psychological wounds with migraines and stomachaches, deeply angry and resentful. We are so competent. No one knows our pain; no one feels our pain. Fighting the demons of the past, alone.

How do we stop these frightening feelings that linger forever? As much as we try to suck it up, not let it show, we writhe in pain. When something stirs our memories, our body responds. Years later we find ourselves hardwired to responses based on the stress of years earlier. We are told to control our anger! Anger at not letting our emotions show?

The worst part is we love our abusers. Most often, the men who take advantage of us live with the family. Fathers and brothers, stepfathers, the boyfriend. Many never see justice; they are not made accountable for their lecherous and abusive ways. The crime goes unpunished.

Instead, the prey, the victims of these men, are the ones who are punished. Children become oppositional and defiant. Woman become depressed and emotionally charged. We lose trust and become hypervigilant, constantly reading people to anticipate the danger. After a while, this becomes wearing. Always on the alert, watching for the next attack. Wholesome relationships require love and trust. Our relationships turn troubled because we are ashamed and embarrassed to admit we were taken advantage of, and we can't get over it.

Once we start the conversation, we can heal. If we keep these feelings deep inside, we forever carry the torment.

Trauma has many tiers. The first layer, the original event. The second level; invalidation of our situation by those around us. People deny a problem exists because they rarely connect emotional and behavioral problems to traumatic events. The third level comes from entities like therapists, the legal system, and the medical community.

The medical community treats physical ailments and doesn't address the situations causing them. The legal system prefers to incarcerate people rather than enroll them in counseling. Up until now, the mental health system has seen symptoms produced from trauma as a mental disorder, but are finally beginning to change their mind and see trauma as a physical manifestation of memories.

What should we do to rid ourselves of these persistent and ugly demons? There is nothing honorable or smart about staying in an abusive relationship. If the relationship is so verbally and emotionally abusive, the best thing may be to cut the ties. Go your separate ways. The only exception is if he is a stalker and you are better off sleeping with the enemy. In this case, you must quietly and secretly take steps to rid yourself of this abusive, controlling man. Most important, stay safe.

If you wish your relationship to be saved, it must be an agreement between both of you to become actively involved in healing old injuries. Healing together can be a powerful building block by developing an understanding and compassion of how one another feels. The critical step is to stop the fighting, the abusive words, the anger. Then, and only then, is healing possible.

Therapies that stir up memories by reliving the moment make things worse. Several treatment modalities such as eye movement desensitization and reprogramming (EMDR), neurofeedback, and trauma processing work better than most. However, you cannot treat the mind without treating the body. The mantra is old-hat, but worth repeating. Healing is not complete without proper nutrition and physical activity.

Exercise is highly overrated. Excessive workouts damage muscle and release high amounts of cortisol into the system. Extreme athletes often end up with autoimmune diseases because they push their bodies beyond the limit. Moderation is the key in all activities; eating, sleeping, exercise and leisure time. Relaxing physical movement and eating foods that put minimal strain on the body are as necessary as brain-calming mental exercises.

Healing the Past

We cope by learning to live with our demons and find respite from the pain. An alcoholic is often someone with a troubled childhood who is unconsciously searching for anything that can comfort his brain.

Music soothes the savage beast. Playing a musical instrument or singing works different parts of the brain, takes attention away from troubles, and brings on a state of bliss and contentment. The problems in the world fade away, and there are no worries until the moment is over. Other art forms that lock the mind for any length of time, such as drawing, dancing, acting, or writing, also engages the body and lets the mind rest.

Bilateral movement, working both sides of the body equally, engages the neurologic system and balances things out. Injuries to the mind and body create blockages in the body. The Ancient Chinese believed blocked energy flow (qi) created disease.

Practicing martial arts, Qigong, or tai chi, reaps many benefits. Five minutes a day of Qigong breathing and visualization melds the mind with the body. Traditional martial arts teach self-defense and self-control with the goal of achieving balance and harmony through meditation, visualization, and physical exercise.

Neurofeedback (NFB) rewires the networks in the nervous system while cognitively retraining the brain. During NFB, wire leads attached to the scalp transmit signals from the brain to a computer program and searches out misfiring neurons, either calming them or rerouting the impulses. The results are quite amazing. Neurofeedback reduces the panic and puts out the fires. Relief at last!

Eye movement desensitization and reprocessing (EMDR) works the body bilaterally with tapping or sound. The client experiences their traumatic event as if watching a movie, while the therapist carefully monitors both pleasant and unpleasant reactions. An EMDR set lasts a minute or two, and with each set throughout the session, the unpleasant memories are processed and replaced with pleasant memories. This technique works well for both children and adults.

Rewiring the brain builds new pathways; rebuilding takes time. The body will remember forgotten memories, and will re-experience some aspects of the event. After a time, the mind will clear, new thought patterns will emerge, and the world will look brighter. When perceptions change, worldview changes. Hypervigilance and panic become a manageable roar.

Is it possible to fully heal from deep emotional scarring? Yes, if the event is processed soon afterward. Flashbacks and panic in the first month to six weeks after the trauma are common. After that, these unresolved feelings become a pattern and develop into post-traumatic stress disorder (PTSD). Remember the discussions on biology and neurology? There is nothing mentally-ill about PTSD. It is a physical manifestation. The body is out of balance. Unbalanced biology and neurology create PTSD.

Treatment involves clearing out the clogged energy channels of the body/mind/soul. If left untreated, PTSD will eventually evolve into serious illnesses such as dementia, delusions, mania, and Alzheimer's disease.

Healing from abuse is the same as healing from any other addiction. Addicts must leave their addicted friends behind. A recovering junky will not heal with his friends hounding him for more drugs. If you are serious about breaking an addiction, you must remove yourself from that environment completely.

"But I love him, I love my family, I can't just walk away." No, we can't, can we? And that is why we stay.

Family Counseling

The object of this treatise is to save families, not destroy them further. People need each other in a crisis. Separating the family during a domestic dispute creates a further rift in the relationship.

Talking about elephants in the room means asking questions. "Why are you this way? Why are you abusive? What causes these outbursts? What can we do to change things?" If people are truly willing to change and to create a better family environment, they will honestly answer these questions and do what is necessary to resolve the past. The only way we can stop this epidemic that has seized our world is with prevention. Abuse stops with me.

We stop abuse by refusing to allow it. We do not deny it; we bring it into the open. When our child comes home from school and tells us about her bully, we do something about it. We watch our actions and words and refrain from abusing others. We respect life, and practice daily the virtues of kindness, compassion, and understanding.

****

How to Have a Successful Life #2

1. Eliminate the backstabbers and negative people.
2. Be pleasant, not catty. Your words reflect who you are. Speak kindly of others.
3. Live your life the way you want. You are in control.
4. Accomplishments come from within. Don't depend on others to get you where you need to go.
5. Never give up. Let your higher power guide you.

****

Afterthoughts

Even though we take different roads to ascend the
wooded mountain,
each of us can achieve our goal
and appreciate the moon when we reach the top.

~Chinese Proverb~

PTSD. YOU CAN'T FIGHT, AND YOU CAN'T FLEE. Stuckedness. A made-up term to describe the feeling. The mind/body/soul can handle only so much. Our psyches have a built-in defense mechanism to induce the mind to shutdown.

In the previous pages, we discussed events leading to PTSD. I wish you enlightenment; to balance your life, your mind, and your soul; and be free of horrors of the past. There is no need to live with hypervigilance and fear.

Life is 90% mental attitude. Bad days happen. The choice lies in how we handle them.

Positive imagining and gratitude are two ways to improve even the worst day. Faith the size of a mustard seed moves mountains. Believe in your goals and be grateful for what you have. Calming the psyche and forgiving self and others also helps the day go better.

Positive imagining. To visualize means to see the subject, the dream, the goal, in the mind's eye. If deep dark thoughts become a habit, happy, cheery thoughts are also a habit. People who have a positive outlook arise eager and happy to meet the oncoming day.

They see problems as challenges needing to be solved. Happiness permeates their being!

How do they do it?

People who are born with a golden purse never want for anything. Ironically, the happiest people seem to be those who experienced intense adversity. They lived through their experience and used their knowledge as a guide for the future. In short – they learned to appreciate life through some near catastrophe and discovered gratitude.

Gratitude. A simple way to change your mood. Feelings of hatefulness and gratefulness cannot exist at the same time. Look around! Give thanks for what you have.

The first step to positive imagining is gratitude. Practice seeing the energy, the pathway of qi, surging through your body. Visualize as if the desire has happened. See the check in hand, experience the joy of receiving it. Become one in the moment.

The trick is in believing and having a positive attitude. Know with all your heart that you will realize your desires. Practice the patience to give your dreams time to manifest themselves. The physical plane, bound in time, works slower than the mental plane, which produces results in a heartbeat. Every time you imagine your goal and place it firmly in your heart, you are one step closer to realizing your dream. It takes time, and you learn patience.

Realizing dreams are like building a house. Before the carpenter lays the first piece of lumber, the house became a reality in the builder's mind. The house started as an idea, "I want to build a house," and grew from there. In time, he built a house.

Dreams and desires are no different. We get what we want by laying a solid foundation. First, we see in our mind what we want.

We fail because we lose sight of the goal. We get side-tracked, and the picture fades. The blueprints of our dreams sit on the shelf and gather dust. Forgotten.

The Psyche. Think of the psyche as divided into two parts - the internal and the external. The external mind is the monkey-mind. This mind never stops working, directing the flow of thinking, acting as the command center of our daily living.

The internal self is a calm, still pool, brightly reflecting the moonlight - stillness all around. Going to this place in our minds reaches for our souls - touching who we truly are. The majority of us live in the external world. And beyond this world in our mind, of course, is the real stimulus: People. Drama.

To achieve perfect healing, first, the abuse must stop. Wounds continually ripped open will not heal. Secondly, go to your lovely, calm, quiet place in your mind every time a stressor hits. Make it a conscious practice, and soon calmness will become a good habit. Rather than letting the brain spin randomly every time danger threatens, teach the mind to stay calm and centered. Keeping calm takes practice. Another attitude that takes practice is forgiveness.

Forgiveness. Letting go of hatred and grudges. Letting things run their course and feeling abundant in your surroundings. Keep your eyes on your goal and practice calm. Easier said than done? Yes, it is. All you have to do is ... Believe it. Healing is possible.

Once you step on the path, you will be amazed.

The steps for healing are different for everyone. No single mixture works for all, and no single modality will work in isolation. You will find a combination of ways to make a daily habit. You will gain satisfaction and encouragement from having a game plan and sticking to it. Celebrate the little things. Be sure to praise yourself! Treat yourself with kindness and others will be kinder to you.

Life is a celebration - but those of us in trauma do not appreciate the fireworks! Accepting limitations are critical. When you take control of your life, your limitations become a gift. A gift because unreasonable expectations no longer exist.

Healthy and happy. A goal reached by setting boundaries, choosing the right teammates and treating people with kindness: A combination that will never go wrong.

Blessings, dear readers. May you walk this earth in peace and harmony.

Be the Change that You Want to See in the World
~Mahatma Gandhi~

A Child Learns What He Lives

IF A CHILD LIVES WITH CRITICISM, HE LEARNS TO CONDEMN.

IF A CHILD LIVES WITH HOSTILITY, HE LEARNS TO FIGHT.

IF A CHILD LIVES WITH SHAME, HE LEARNS TO FEEL GUILTY.

IF A CHILD LIVES WITH TOLERANCE, HE LEARNS TO BE PATIENT.

IF A CHILD LIVES WITH ENCOURAGEMENT, HE LEARNS CONFIDENCE.

IF A CHILD LIVES WITH PRAISE, HE LEARNS TO APPRECIATE.

IF A CHILD LIVES WITH FAIRNESS, HE LEARNS JUSTICE.

IF A CHILD LIVES WITH SECURITY, HE LEARNS TO HAVE FAITH.

IF A CHILD LIVES WITH APPROVAL, HE LEARNS TO LIKE HIMSELF.

IF A CHILD LIVES WITH ACCEPTANCE AND FRIENDSHIP,

HE LEARNS LOVE IS IN THE WORLD.

~Dorothy Law Nolte

Bibliography

Brethnach, S. B. (1998). *Something more. Excavating your authentic self.* NY. Time Warner.

Carnegie, D. (1988). *How to win friends and influence people.* (Revised). New York. Simon and Shuster.

de Becker, G. (1999). *The gift of fear and other survival signals that protect us from danger.* New York. Dell Publishing.

Fanton, E.; Foley, H.P.: Kampen, N.B; Pomeroy, S.B.: Shapiron, H.A. (1999*). Women in the classical world.* New York. Oxford Press

Goleman, D. (2006). *Social Intelligence. The new science of human relationships.* USA. Bantam Books.

Harris, G. (2005). *Your heart knows the answer. How to trust yourself and make the choices right for you. Ceremonies, prayers, and affirmations.* Novato, CA. New World Library.

Hanson, R. Ph.D.; Mendius, R., MD. (2009). *The practical neuroscience of Buddha's brain. Happiness, love, wisdom.* Oakland, CA. Harbinger Publications.

Lang, D. (1999). *The new secrets of charisma. How to discover and unleash your hidden powers.* Lincolnwood, IL. Contemporary Books. (p. 13).

Lawrence, P.R.; Nohria, N. (2002). *Driven. How human nature shapes our choices.* San Francisco, CA. Jossey-Bass. (p.86).

Levine, P. (2010). *In an unspoken voice.* Berkeley, CA. North Atlantic Books. (p. 48).

Levine, P. (1997). *Waking the tiger. Healing trauma. How the body releases trauma and stores goodness.* Berkeley, CA. North Atlantic Books.

Scott, S. K. (2006). *The richest man who ever lived. King Solomon's secrets to success, wealth, and happiness.* USA. Doubleday.

van der Kolk, B. M.D. (2014). *The body keeps the score. Brain, mind and body in the healing of trauma.* NY. Penguin Books.

Acknowledgements

MANY PEOPLE HAVE CONTRIBUTED to my book, too many to mention here. Ten years ago, there wasn't much literature on the subject, and I am indebted to the authors and researchers who opened the doors leading to understanding trauma. A great thank you to my family for their patience, for their helpful advice, and for putting up with the long hours of writing and learning to publish. This book would not be possible without the support of my PLTI family and my Sensei. Much gratitude to you all.

About the Author

WOMEN OFTEN CAME TO MY SELF-DEFENSE CLASSES to learn to protect themselves from an abusive mate. Their stories are silently interwoven into these pages. In 2012, when taking a research class for my master's degree, I discovered the newly-released ACES study, which confirmed my suspicions of the effects childhood abuse had on adults. This was the answer I needed to finish my book.

This treatise is a combination of many years of hard-won wisdom, working with veterans, personal experience, and research. I believe that by practicing kindness and compassion, and through prevention and education, we can halt the spread of violence in our world.

Please see the back pages for an excerpt of my second book: *Take the Quantum Leap into Abundance. A manual for better living.*

Contact:

cpickett@wyoming.com

ALSO BY THE AUTHOR

Take the Quantum Leap

~INTO ABUNDANCE~

A GUIDE TO THE GOOD LIFE

C.W. PICKETT

Mu Shin Press

If you have not linked yourself to true emptiness
You will never understand
The Art of Peace

You must never confuse faith that you will
prevail in the end – which you can never afford to
lose – with the discipline to confront the most brutal
facts of your current reality, whatever that might be.

~Admiral James Stockdale~

FORETHOUGHTS

WHAT IS ABUNDANCE?

HEALTHY, WEALTHY, AND WISE

Do not fail to learn from the pure voice
of an ever-flowing mountain stream
splashing over the rocks.

~The Art of Peace~

ABUNDANCE.

WHAT IS IT? HOW DO YOU FIND IT?

HOW DO YOU KNOW WHEN YOU HAVE FOUND IT?

In the late 1980's, there was a television series called The *Quantum Leap.* Doctor Sam Beckett devised a time-travel machine and was forced to use it before it was thoroughly tested. The machine backfired, and he found himself in another body, traveling from life to life, looking for his way back home. His one helper was Al, a holographic image seen only by Dr. Beckett.

This book is not about time travel, nor is it science fiction. When a person travels from one level of consciousness to another, they are taking the Quantum Leap, a giant leap of faith into their metaphorical "other world;" the world that exists exclusively in personal dreams and ambitions.

Where is this other world, this life of abundance? People are searching for truths, for a way of living not fraught with violence and drama. Many books are written on how to live a better life, nearly to the point of information overload. This book is different. You cannot think yourself thin, nor can you dream your way into riches. The work ethic of "no work, no food," applies to making your life better, as well. If you do not apply the energy and time necessary to build a better life for yourself, you will not succeed. The ideas presented were gathered over the years through education, research, experience, and the school of hard knocks.

Intentionally written to be thought provoking, my book is called a manual because it is not intended to be a sit-down one-time read for a couple of hours. It is my goal that you stop and reflect on an insight, or perhaps a quote will help you along the way. The ideas presented here have helped me through difficult times, and I hope you will refer to my book often, just as I did while writing it.

My books are intended to pass on worthwhile knowledge that readers can apply to their lives. Knowledge is useless unless passed on. Without sharing what we have learned, education and knowledge sit in our brains and stagnates. What you read in these pages is a compilation of universal truths, of knowledge, passed down through time; truths that light the dark corners of our souls.

Let us begin the journey with this simple statement.

Your thoughts make you. Think positive thoughts and you will have a positive life.

Much is written on the subject. Through the centuries, many people have told us our thoughts lead the way: Norman V. Peale, Aristotle, William James, Myomoto Musashi, Admiral James Stockdale, Maya Angelou, and Mother Theresa are examples. People such as these discover universal truths and pass them on as their legacy. For the purposes of our reading, they are called Quantum People. Their experiences led them to abundance and self-fulfillment - their lives a bright beacon for us to follow.

"But wait!" you ask. "If thinking positive thoughts is all it takes, then why is there poverty and chronic illness? Why have people suffered through the ages with slavery and oppression?" If all you had to do was wish, would these conditions exist? What poor man hasn't dreamed of wealth? What dying man hasn't yearned for a return to his health and vigor?

Visualize your dream, imagine it coming to life. Is it an impossible dream to see yourself thin? Is it impossible to find happiness? Are we fooling ourselves by imagining a better life is waiting for us if we try a little harder? How true is this advice the Quantum People give? For instance, is it possible to *Think and Grow Rich*?

To write this book, these questions, and many others, called for answers. There are many components to living a successful life, and each person's definition of success is different. The path you chose is your path, you find people along the way who are compatible with you, but the path is yours and only yours. You can make certain choices, but some choices are made for you, whether you like them or not. How you rebound from unpleasant choices or outcomes is how you define your life.

All it takes to start a dream is to put a thought into your brain and then forget about it. Physical motion measures our sense of time, but in the universe, and therefore our thoughts, time has no boundaries or measurement. Life's lessons happen when we are receptive to the point, and not a moment earlier. "Why didn't I think of that sooner?" Now is when your mind is receptive to the idea and you didn't have enough information to act "sooner."

Have you ever done the exercise, "If I were to die in six months, what could I do with the time I have remaining?" One of the items on my list was to write a book, which I wrote down, tucked the paper away, and forgot about. Fifteen years later, after publishing my first book, I rediscovered the paper. Unknown to me at the time, a thought was anchored in my brain and left to grow on its own. Over the years, this commitment stayed as a niggling voice in my head, the ideas turned into words on paper, and one day, a book appeared. At the time of the original thought, there was no time limit, and not even a very strong belief it might happen. The book did not write itself, of course, and it was my physical manifestations of researching the topic and putting words on paper. Nevertheless, a remote dream turned into an idea strong enough to weather life's challenges and become real.

Do not give up when life isn't happening on your time schedule. Your job is to plant the seeds and then let the Universe do the work. Your idea will massage and grow in your subconscious until one day it will become a reality. But only if you give it room to grow. If you plead, beg, and grovel to make it work, your idea slip away.

Remember! Life is an adventure, a process. A process that takes a lifetime. The recipe involves positive thoughts, gratitude, visualizing, faith, and *patience.* Positive thinking in and of itself does not produce a single result. What produces results is action. As we will see in Chapter 5, Positive Self-Imaging, the bridge between thought and action, is discipline.

Discipline of mind and body, of habits, and of daily living. When thinking positively, a person uses discipline to reign in the negative thoughts when they start. There is no room for "I will never ..." "I will never get well." "I will never walk again." "I will never..."

It is not fully possible to absolutely, without question, control our thoughts and our destiny. It is wrong to assume we completely control our lives. If you are living in trauma, you may see the world as scary. Thoughts alone will not change that. You will not wake up one day and think your way positive. Be wary of the charlatans who sell the idea of "thinking without action."

You are not a failure if you cannot think yourself rich. People fail when striving toward a fulfilling life because they do not have the knowledge or the tools for success.

My book has practical and simple techniques for developing skills that lead to living an abundant life. There is a chapter on how to improve your self-image, another on the importance of listening. No book of this kind is complete without a chapter on meditation, but here you will find a method different from the rest, and it only takes a few minutes. You will find yourself doing this simple, calming practice whenever you have the chance. Now you can drift off to sleep with your last thoughts of qi, your life force, slowly meandering throughout your body. With practice over time, you will be able to use qi energy to heal hot spots and relieve pain.

You will read about people who overcame their adversity and turned it into a peak experience, a life-defining moment, and lived a long and fulfilling life. We will explore choices that are not choices, the cycle of needs we live by, and why some people are more resilient than others. Each chapter focuses on a person or group of people whose faith gives us hope that anyone who wants to can find their authentic life.

The people in this book are real. They arrived at their philosophy of better living through trial and tribulation. The idea is to present their legacies, and by following their path, the reader may also find abundance and self-fulfillment.

What is good living? How do you know when you have found abundance? Let us first look at choices that are not really choices.

www.ingramcontent.com/pod-product-compliance
Lightning Source LLC
Chambersburg PA
CBHW030836300326
41935CB00036B/328